Let's eat Dinner

KU-655-509

Clare Hibbert

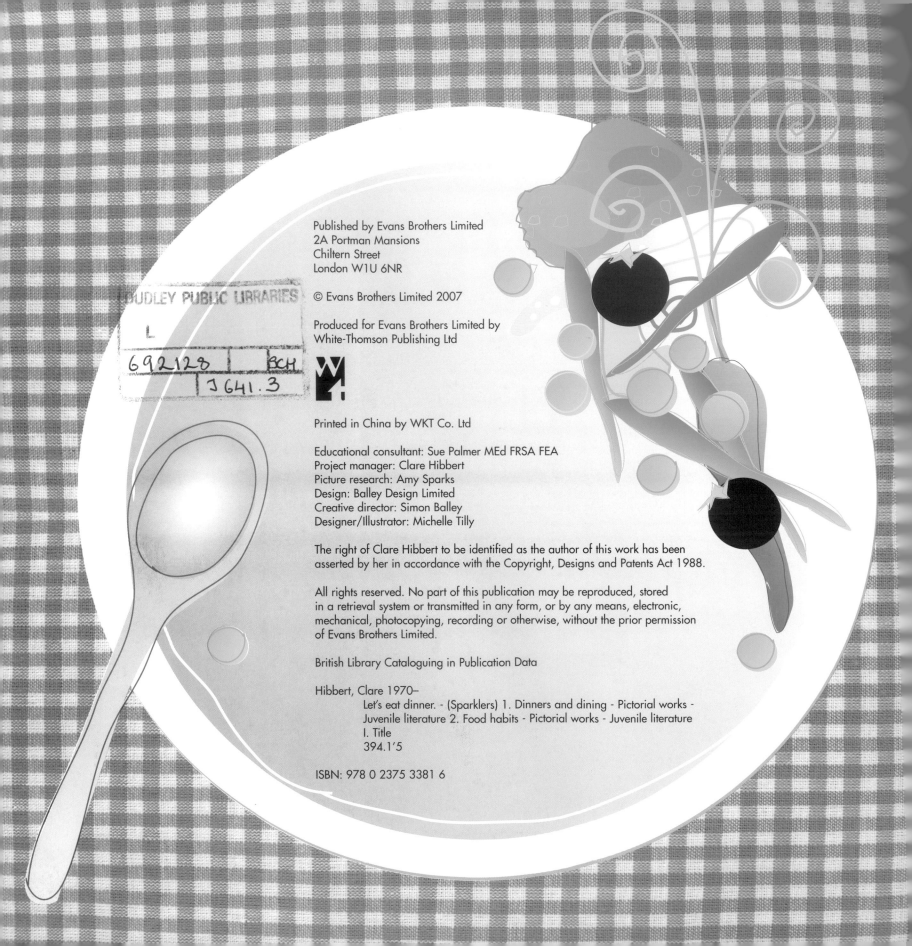

Published by Evans Brothers Limited
2A Portman Mansions
Chiltern Street
London W1U 6NR

© Evans Brothers Limited 2007

Produced for Evans Brothers Limited by
White-Thomson Publishing Ltd

Printed in China by WKT Co. Ltd

Educational consultant: Sue Palmer MEd FRSA FEA
Project manager: Clare Hibbert
Picture research: Amy Sparks
Design: Balley Design Limited
Creative director: Simon Balley
Designer/Illustrator: Michelle Tilly

The right of Clare Hibbert to be identified as the author of this work has been
asserted by her in accordance with the Copyright, Designs and Patents Act 1988.

All rights reserved. No part of this publication may be reproduced, stored
in a retrieval system or transmitted in any form, or by any means, electronic,
mechanical, photocopying, recording or otherwise, without the prior permission
of Evans Brothers Limited.

British Library Cataloguing in Publication Data

Hibbert, Clare 1970–
    Let's eat dinner. - (Sparklers) 1. Dinners and dining - Pictorial works -
    Juvenile literature 2. Food habits - Pictorial works - Juvenile literature
    I. Title
    394.1'5

ISBN: 978 0 2375 3381 6

DUDLEY PUBLIC LIBRARIES

L

692128   BCH
          J 641.3

DUDLEY SCHOOLS LIBRARY
AND INFORMATION SERVICE

Schools Library and Infomation Services

S00000692128

Contents

Dinner time

This book is about dinner.

4

What time do you eat your dinner?

5

Getting ready

How do you help

make dinner?

tablecloth

Who sets the table in your house?

7

splosh

Rice **grows** in hot, rainy countries.

broccoli

cauliflower

pepper

How do you like them cooked?

11

Food from the sea

Which fish do you
like to eat?

mussel

This is a tasty fish stew.

All kinds of meat

Butchers sell meat.

16

lamb kebab

What's your favourite meat dinner?

17

Desserts

When do you like cold desserts?

18

apple pie

When do you like hot desserts?

19

Make it: Raita

Mix these things together
to make raita.

- cumber ✓
- plain yoghurt ✓
- ground cumin ✓
- lemon juice ✓

naan

20

Raita tastes good with curry and naan bread.

Notes for adults

Sparklers books are designed to support and extend the learning of young children. The books' high-interest subjects link in to the Early Years curriculum and beyond. Find out more about Early Years and reading with children from the National Literacy Trust (www.literacytrust.org.uk).

Themed titles
Let's eat Dinner is one of four **Food We Eat** titles that explore food and meals from around the world. The other titles are:
Let's eat Breakfast   Let's eat Lunch   Celebration Food

Areas of learning
Each **Food We Eat** title helps to support the following Foundation Stage areas of learning:
Personal, Social and Emotional Development
Communication, Language and Literacy
Mathematical Development
Knowledge and Understanding of the World
Creative Development

Reading together
When sharing this book with younger children, take time to explore the pictures together. Encourage children by asking them to find, identify, count or describe different objects. Point out different colours or textures.

Allow quiet spaces in your reading so that children can ask questions or repeat your words. Try pausing mid-sentence so children can predict the next word. This sort of participation develops early reading skills.

Follow the words with your finger as you read them aloud. The main text is in Infant Sassoon, a clear, friendly font specially designed for children learning to read and write. The labels and sound effects on the pages add fun, engage the reader and give children the opportunity to distinguish between different levels of communication. Where appropriate, labels, sound effects or main text may be presented in phonic spelling. Encourage children to imitate the sounds.

As you read the book, you can also take the opportunity to talk about the book itself with appropriate vocabulary, such as "page", "cover", "back", "front", "photograph", "label" and "page number".

You can also extend children's learning by using the books as a springboard for discussion and further activities. There are a few suggestions on the facing page.

22

Pages 4–5: Dinner time

Encourage children to keep a food diary, either as a group or individually. Divide a big piece of paper into seven sections, one for each day of the week. Encourage children to draw, paint or stick photos of what they ate for dinner on each day.

Pages 6–7: Getting ready

Make mini pizzas from homemade salt dough, then bake and paint. Use as a prop in a pretend pizzeria, where children can role play being cooks, serving staff or customers.

Pages 8–9: Rice

Fill a large box (or sand table) with rice which children can explore and pour using funnels, spoons, scoops and cups. For multicoloured rice, shake up uncooked white rice, food colouring and a little water or white spirit in a sealed plastic bag, then air-dry on a tray for a few hours.

Pages 10–11: Fresh vegetables

If you have outdoor space, grow vegetables. Peas are rewarding, since most children like to eat them. Otherwise, grow carrot tops. Put each carrot top on wet cotton wool on a saucer and wait for the leaves to sprout. Encourage children to count the fronds or even chart the growth.

Pages 12–13: Pasta and noodles

Sitting alongside a child at the computer, type "pasta shapes" into an internet search engine. Print off reference of different shapes and their names, which the children can copy to make their own pasta poster.

Pages 14–15: Food from the sea

Put on some 'watery' music, then ask children to dance while role playing different marine animals, such as crab, shark or octopus.

Pages 16–17: All kinds of meat

Create a mural of shopfronts. Write the name of each shop – for example, butcher, baker, greengrocer, jeweller – and then fill its window with a collage of 'produce' (artworks made by the children).

Pages 18–19: Desserts

Find out what children's favourite desserts are, and compile a recipe book illustrated with paintings by the children.

Pages 20–21: Make it: Raita

Make basic raita and then divide it into small portions, each with an additional flavouring such as chopped coriander, raisins or grated apple. Arrange a blind tasting and see which flavours the children like best.

Index

Picture acknowledgements:
Alamy: 12 (Image State), 15 (Food Folio); **Corbis:** 17 (Hall/Photocuisine); **Evans:** 4-5 (Gareth Boden); **Getty:** cover (Foodcollection), 6 (Flynn Larsen), 7 (Stephanie Rausser/Taxi), 8 (Altrendo), 16 (Lee Strickland/Taxi), 19 (Angela Wyant/Stone); **iStockphoto:** cover tablecloth, 2-3, 22-24 (Gaffera), cover sky, 22-24 (Judy Foldetta), 11 (Bluestocking), 18 (David Hernandez); **Photolibrary:** 9 (Patrick Syder), 10 (Index Stock Imagery), 13 (Foodpix), 20-21 (Andrew Sydenham); **WT-Pix:** 14.